Step Families

Sarah Levete

Franklin Watts
London • Sydney

Paperback edition published
in 2006.

© Aladdin Books Ltd 2004

Designed and produced by
Aladdin Books Ltd
2/3 Fitzroy Mews
London W1T 6DF

First published in Great Britain
in 2004 by
Franklin Watts
338 Euston Road
London NW1 3BH

Picture research:
Brian Hunter Smart
Editors: Jim Pipe & Rebecca Pash
The consultant, Vicky Leach, is
Family Mediation & Children's
Support Services Adviser for the
children's charity NCH.

The publishers would like
to acknowledge that the
photographs reproduced in this
book have been posed by
models or have been obtained
from photographic agencies.

A CIP record for this book is
available from the British Library.

Dewey Classification: 306.874'7

Printed in Malaysia

Contents

"What is a step family?"

What is your family like? Do you have lots of sisters and brothers? Perhaps your family is just you and one of your parents. Some children live with their grandparents.

You may be part of a step family, or you may know someone who is part of a step family. All families are different and a step family is just one type of family.

A step family is just one type of family.

A step family is formed when one parent meets a new partner. They might live together or get married. One or both of them may already have children.

This book helps you to understand what it means to be part of a step family. It discusses how a child may feel when a step family is formed. It talks about the challenges and rewards of being part of a step family.

You may live in a step family, or maybe someone in your class is part of a step family.

"How does a step family come together?"

Families change when there is a loss or a break-up. The loss may be the death of one parent. A break-up happens if parents decide to live apart.

When this happens, one or both parents may meet another partner and live with him or her. This creates a step family.

A step family can form after a parent dies and the other parent meets a new partner.

It's important to remember that whatever the reason for parents being apart, it is never a child's fault.

Children who form part of a step family will have been part of another family, their first family. Babies or young children may be part of a step family. Others may become part of a step family as teenagers.

Did you know...

There are different kinds of parents. The mum and dad who made you are biological or birth parents. They may also be called blood parents.

Whatever happens, they will always be your birth parents. Some children, who also have step-parents, call their birth parents their "real" or "natural" mum and dad.

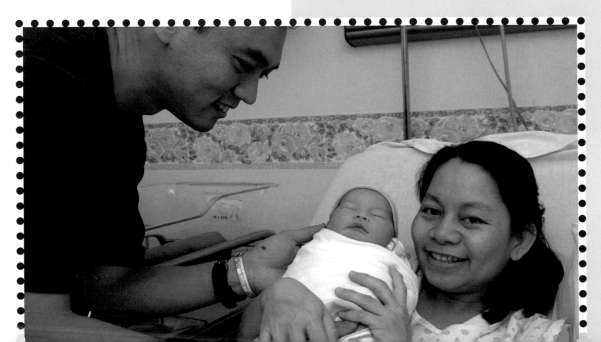

"What's a step family like?"

A step family can be large or small. Some children may belong to two step families.

Just like any other family, step families come in all shapes and sizes. In some step families, the birth and step-parent may be of the same sex. Some parents marry, and others decide simply to live together.

A step family may be made up of one child and the birth and step-parent. Or, if your step-parent has his or her own children, these become your step-brothers and -sisters.

If the birth and step-parent have a baby together, this is your half-brother or -sister.

If both birth parents set up home with new partners, you may find yourself with two step families!

Don't forget, you'll also have two new sets of aunts, uncles and grandparents. It can get quite complicated!

Think about it

If your birth and step-parent have a baby together, you may worry that it will stop you from being special. But nothing is likely to change your parents' love for you. Talking to both your birth and step parent can reassure you. And having a baby brother or sister can be fun!

"What happens in a step family?"

When a family breaks up, for whatever reason, there are lots of confusing feelings to deal with. A step family then coming together can create even more difficult feelings. There can be lots of diffcult decisions to make, such as who lives with whom.

Each family situation is different. Some children are very close to and may live with their step family. Others have little or no contact.

As a step family comes together, there are lots of issues to deal with.

Some children can choose how much they are involved and others are given no choice. This can be hard to accept.

Explain clearly to your parents how you feel. It may not change anything, but it will help you deal with the situation.

Think about it

A step family is no more or less of a family than any other type of family. But a step family does face more challenges. Everyone has to adjust to the break-up of the first family and the coming together of the new family. It can be hard, but in time everyone can enjoy being part of a step family.

"Do step families always live together?"

Some children live with the step family for all or most of the time. This may mean moving to a new home or perhaps moving to a new school in a new area.

Other children visit the step family at weekends. If so, it helps to feel part of the family by having a special place in the step family's house for your belongings.

Some children move house to live with the step family. Others visit the step family occasionally.

Living with one family for half the week and the step family for the rest of the week is fun, but also quite challenging!

It's not easy to organise your belongings between two houses or to remember the different household rules. Chat to your parents if you are finding it difficult.

My story

"I live with my step family and see my dad in the holidays. I had to move house and change schools. At first I missed my friends but I keep in touch through email. One of my old friends is coming to stay for a weekend and I've made some new friends at school too."
Charlie

"Does everything change in a step family?"

Sometimes, everything in a step family feels different. Your step family may be from a different culture or have different religious beliefs. There may be new rules about watching TV or doing homework, or you may not be used to the food. These things can make you feel as if you don't fit in. But in time, everything will seem less strange and you will feel more relaxed.

You may not be used to the way your step family does things.

Try to show consideration and respect for any differences in your step family. Tolerance and understanding will make it easier for everyone to settle in.

Adapting to change takes time. It's confusing at first, but once you have got used to it, change can bring good feelings too.

Think about it

Becoming part of a step family doesn't change your first family's feelings towards you. They will carry on loving you. And you can carry on loving your birth parents and brothers and sisters, just as before.

"How does it feel to be part of a step family?"

For many, becoming part of a step family creates difficult feelings. Children may still be upset by the break-up of the first family or be grieving for a lost parent. It is common to feel confused, lonely or sad.

You may feel angry towards other family members. You may think that nobody is interested in you or feel as if you don't belong. You may miss your other parent. All of these feelings are natural.

It is common to feel confused, angry or upset. In time, these feelings pass.

It's easier to deal with feelings if you can express them. Try writing them down, or talk to your parents or close friends.

Whatever is going on at home, try not to let it affect everything else. Keep up with any activities you enjoy, such as playing with friends.

My story

"I missed Mum so much after she died. I was angry with dad for meeting Jill, my stepmum. I didn't want a new mum. It was like I didn't belong anywhere. I used to argue with everyone. Talking to my teacher really helped. Now I tell dad and Jill how I feel. I still miss Mum but I've accepted the situation now." Sasha

"Do I have to like my step-parent?"

Just because your birth parent loves your step-parent, it doesn't mean you will feel the same! Try not to worry if you don't like your step-parent. It takes time to get to know anyone.

In the meantime, learn how to get on with each other as well as possible. Avoid comparing your step- and birth parent. Everyone is different and has different ways of doing things.

You may not like your step parent at first, but try to give them a chance.

You may think your step-parent is trying to replace your birth parent. This is probably not the case, but your step-parent may be trying too hard to make friends with you.

Some children call their step-parent by his or her first name. Others call him or her "Mum" or "Dad". Decide with your step-parent what feels right for all of you.

Think about it

Try to show respect and kindness to your step-parent, even if you don't feel happy about the situation.

Remember, he or she may also feel anxious about getting to know you. Your step-parent may not have looked after children before, so be patient!

"What about step-brothers and -sisters?"

Just as you are joining a new family, so too may your stepbrothers and -sisters. They probably feel equally unsure and anxious!

If you are not used to sharing your parent's attention, you may feel jealous or resentful towards a new stepbrother or -sister.

Sharing your parent's attention with a stepbrother or -sister can be hard.

Yet, nothing will change the special love between you and your birth parent.

Ask your birth parent if you can spend some time alone together. If you are used to living in a quiet house with plenty of room, you may find it hard living in a noisy, crowded house.

Talk to your parents. They may not be able to magic a big quiet house for you, but they may be able to arrange some space and quiet time for each child.

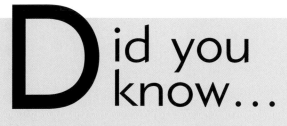

Did you know...

There's good news! Step-brothers and -sisters can be great fun. They are ready-made new friends.

Older children can help you out with homework, and younger ones will really look up to you!

"What about my 'real' parent?"

Some children, especially those who live with the step family most of the time, feel anxious about, and miss, their other birth parent. But remember that you can still love your mum or dad, even if you live apart.

It's natural to miss your birth parent, but this needn't stop you enjoying time with your step family.

Some parents continue to argue even after separating. It is not fair if you feel caught in the middle and pressurised to take sides. Explain to your parents how this makes you feel.

Many children feel disloyal to the birth parent if they get on with the step-parent. But it's OK to love both sets of parents.

Having a good relationship with your step-parent won't stop you from loving your "real" mum or dad.

Did you know...

Some children feel relieved to be in a step family, especially if their mum or dad is happier. But this can create feelings of guilt and worry about the other birth parent. Remember, you can feel happy as part of a step family and still love your other family.

"Why does it take time for a step family to settle?"

It takes time to adjust to a loss or break-up of parents in the first family, and to accept a new family. Some children may blame their step-parent for their parents' break-up. But this is not fair and won't help the step family settle. Try to give your step-parent a chance.

There may be many ups and downs for everyone. But in time you will come to know and accept each other.

Other children may blame themselves for their parents' separation. But it is never the child's fault. Blaming yourself makes it harder to accept the new situation.

Some children behave badly, hoping to drive their step-parent away. This will make things difficult and unsettled, but it won't make the birth parents get back together.

Try to ignore negative comments from people, such as relatives. Let them know how it makes you feel and ask them not to say things that make it difficult for you.

My story

"Everything was fine until birthdays or Christmas. There were arguments about who I would stay with but now my parents take it in turns. It's taken quite a long time to get used to having two families, but I'm beginning to enjoy it."
Ada

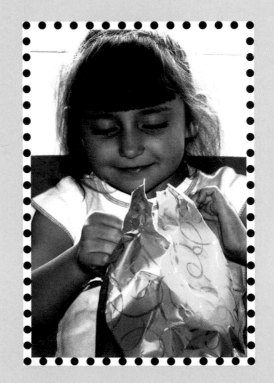

"How can step families sort out problems?"

Bottling up your feelings will not help! Talk to one or both of your parents, or to another person you trust. It may not change the situation, but it will help you feel better. You may find new support and friends in your step-grandparents or relatives. And your birth grandparents will still be there for you.

Talking about problems is the first step towards solving them.

Think about it

There are lots of fairy tales with wicked stepmothers and evil stepfathers. These stories may be fun to read, but they are very unfair on real step-parents.

Being a step-parent is not easy. Remember that stepmums and -dads try hard to fit in and feel at home with their new family.

If there are problems about seeing your birth parent, tell your parents how you feel and what you would like to happen. If they are not able to agree, they can get a mediator to help sort out arrangements. If you feel left out, particularly if step relatives seem only to notice your stepbrothers or -sisters, explain how you feel. They might not be aware of how they are making you feel.

"What makes a happy step family?"

There is no magic way to create an instant happy step family. It takes time and patience. The tips below may help.

① Accept that there will be sad and difficult feelings about the break-up of the first family.

② Be thoughtful about other members of the step family, even if you don't like them much.

③ Talk to family members about how you feel.

In time, members of a step family can learn to enjoy each other's company.

④ Ask your parents for family meetings when everyone can discuss any problems, such as who chooses what to watch on TV. The family can listen to each other and try to sort out the problems together.

⑤ Try to do some things together as a family so that you can share experiences and have shared memories.

Did you know…

There are lots of good things about being in a step family. You'll see your birth parent in a happy relationship. You'll understand that relationships take time to develop. Your step-parent may become a good friend in whom you can confide. You'll have great experiences of new people and ways of living.

"What can I do?"

- Accept that there will be difficult feelings to deal with.
- Talk to others about how you are feeling.
- Remember that it will take time for everyone to adjust.
- Give everyone a chance to settle in. Try to be tolerant and understanding.

- Remember that just like other families, step families fall out with each other and then make friends again.
- If you know another child who is finding it hard to settle in a step family, why not make a special effort to include him or her in your games?

Enjoy the new experiences that a step family gives you.

Books on step families

If you want to read more about step families, try:

What Do You Know About Stepfamilies? by Pete Sanders & Steve Myers (Franklin Watts)
How Do I Feel About My Stepfamily by Julie Johnson (Franklin Watts)

On the Web

These websites are also helpful:

www.itsnotyourfault.org.uk
www.childline.org.uk
www.parentlineplus.org.uk
www.thestepstop.com
www.stepfamily.asn.au

There is lots of useful information about families on the internet.

Contact information

If you want to talk to someone who doesn't know you, these organisations can help:

Childline
Tel: 0800 1111
A 24-hour free helpline for children.

Parentline Plus
520 Highgate Studios,
53-79 Highgate Road, London NW5 1TL
Tel: 020 7284 5500
Helpline: 0800 800 2222
Offers support to families and parents.

Relate
Tel: 0845 456 1310
Helpline: 0845 130 4010
Relate has local offices throughout the United Kingdom.

National Family Mediation
Alexander House,
Telephone Avenue,
Bristol BS1 4BS
Tel: 0117 904 2825
Works to bring separated families closer.

Stepfamily Australia
PO Box 1162, Gawler
South Australia 5118
Tel: 08 8522 7007
Advice and support for step families.

Kids Helpline, Australia
Tel: 1800 55 1800
A 24-hour free helpline for children.

Index

Photocredits

Abbreviations: l-left, r-right, b-bottom, t-top, c-centre, m-middle
All photos supplied by Digital Vision except for:
3tr, 5b, 9b, 27t — Photodisc. 6r — Shane T McCoy/US Navy. 7b — John E Woods/US Navy. 10,
14b, 16b, 18b, 25br — PBD. 13bl — Brand X Pictures. 17tl — Corbis. 22b, 24b, 26b — Jim Pipe.